52-WEEK DEVOTIONAL JOURNAL FOR WOMEN

52-WEEK
DEVOTIONAL
JOURNAL
FOR WOMEN

PROMPTS AND PRAYERS TO REFLECT
AND CONNECT WITH GOD

DEB WOLF

ROCKRIDGE
PRESS

For general information on our other products and services or to obtain technical support, please contact our Customer Care Department within the United States at (866) 744-2665, or outside the United States at (510) 253-0500.

Rockridge Press publishes its books in a variety of electronic and print formats. Some content that appears in print may not be available in electronic books, and vice versa.

Interior and Cover Designer: Karmen Lizzul

Art Producer: Karen Williams

Editor: Lauren O'Neal

Production Editor: Ruth Sakata Corley

ISBN: Print 978-1-64876-008-2

R0

To all the beautiful women God has used to bless and encourage me with His mercy, grace, and love. I am so thankful for you all!

CONTENTS

INTRODUCTION

I used to have a recurring dream. No, not the one where it's time to take an exam and I've never attended the class and can't find the classroom. In this dream, I'd wander around a large home with long hallways lined with doors to rooms I couldn't enter because the doors were locked. I'd grow more anxious and frustrated until I finally woke up feeling restless and confused.

One morning, as I woke up from another hallway visit, I prayed and asked the Lord to show me what it meant. He whispered in response, "That's what your heart looks like to Me." I realized I had hurts behind one door and regrets behind another. Anger hid in one room, while worry was locked in another. I was holding back, but Jesus was asking for my complete trust—everything! He wanted me to unlock the doors and surrender my burdens to Him.

Once I did, God helped me let go of fear, better accept His love, and experience life transformed and peaceful. It's my blessing now to encourage others by sharing the hopeful message of Jesus as an author and speaker.

This dream always reminds me of one of my favorite Bible verses: "Look! I stand at the door and knock. If you hear my voice and open the door, I will come in, and we will share a meal together as friends" (Revelation 3:20). That's my prayer for you with this book. I'm asking God to bless you with peace as you ponder, pray, journal, and open the doors of your heart to Him. May your faith be

strengthened as you learn to trust God to be with you
and help you, no matter what you're dealing with today.

There's no one way to use this book. Each week
offers a devotion and four journal prompts to help you
explore the Scriptures and topics being discussed. The
fourth journal prompt also functions as a prayer prompt
to help you bring what you're thinking and feeling to
God. You can do all your reading and journaling at the
same time every Sunday, spend a few minutes journaling
here and there over the course of the week, or anything
in between. You can keep the book on your bedside table
or carry it around with you. Do whatever helps you
focus your heart and mind on the One who loves you
more than you can imagine. And at the end of the year,
you can flip back through the book to recall what you
were writing about and see how He moved into your life.

I'm really looking forward to spending this time with
you, and I pray God abundantly blesses you as you spend
this time with Him.

IN HIS PRESENCE

My heart has heard you say, "Come and talk with me."
And my heart responds, "Lord, I am coming."
PSALM 27:8

I once asked a group of friends, "How do you picture Jesus when you pray?"

Some said they pictured themselves sitting at Jesus's feet. Others said they imagined Him sitting on the throne or saw themselves kneeling before Him. There were those who held His hand as they took walks with Him, and a few leaned into Him with their head on His shoulder.

I sometimes picture Him sitting quietly in a beautiful field with a smile on His face, inviting me to simply "come and talk." He knows I'm tired and worn out. He knows I've messed up a million times. He knows my weaknesses and failures. And He says, "Let's talk." No judgment. No disappointment. No guilt. Just an invitation to be in His presence.

It's so easy to get lost in the busyness of life, isn't it?

Jesus understands. He was constantly surrounded by people asking Him to tell another story, feed another hungry stomach, or perform another miracle. But He also got away to sit and talk with His Father.

He knew the blessings of comfort, peace, and strength that could only be found in those quiet conversations.

I hope this book encourages countless encounters with your Savior this year.

Take a moment each day this week to hear Him say, "Come and talk with Me." Then picture yourself responding, "Lord, I am coming," as you enter His presence and talk about life.

How do you picture Jesus when you pray?

_____

_____

_____

_____

_____

_____

_____

_____

How does it make you feel that Jesus wants you to "come and talk" with Him? Joyful? Humbled? A little intimidated? Write about it here.

_____

_____

_____

_____

_____

_____

Make a list of times and places you can add prayerful, quiet conversations with Jesus to your day (in the car, in the shower, while you're doing laundry, etc.).

_____

_____

_____

_____

_____

_____

_____

Jesus loves you so much that He wants to hear from you in good times or bad. Write a prayer thanking Him for always wanting you to be in His presence.

_____

_____

_____

_____

_____

_____

_____

_____

_____

WHERE TO TAKE YOUR "WHY?"

Why am I discouraged? Why is my heart so sad?
I will put my hope in God! I will praise him again—
my Savior and my God!
PSALM 42:11

It's so easy to get discouraged, isn't it?

Maybe this isn't how you had imagined this moment in your life. You didn't see yourself stretched so thin with a to-do list that would be impossible to complete even if you worked on it 24/7. If you're like me, you typically feel like you're falling just a bit short of your own expectations, and maybe everyone else's too. You're running as fast as you can, and it still doesn't feel fast enough.

One of my favorite things about the book of Psalms is that David and the other writers were so honest. They expressed their highs and lows, joys and sorrows, and everything in between. They weren't afraid to take their "why" questions to God: Why is life so hard? Why do I keep falling short? Why do I feel so defeated? Why am I discouraged and sad?

I believe that's what God wants us to do. I think He wants us to take our frustrations, doubts, and questions to Him. He wants us to be still and know that He is God (Psalm 46:10).

He wants us to trust that when we don't have the answer, He does. When we're discouraged, He's our hope. When we're falling short, He's our strength.

He wants us to know we can run to Him, however we're feeling, and trust Him to give us everything we need.

Think about the things that are most important to you— activities and responsibilities you wouldn't remove from your to-do list. Make a list of those things.

_____

_____

_____

_____

_____

_____

Now make a list of things that are not as important and that can be removed from your to-do list.

_____

_____

_____

_____

_____

_____

_____

Think about times when you've been discouraged and remember how God reached out to strengthen and encourage you. Write about one of those times here.

_____

_____

_____

_____

_____

What has you frustrated right now? Write it down here. Be honest! Then thank God for the times He's encouraged you and ask Him to help you again with the frustration(s) you're facing at the moment.

_____

_____

_____

_____

_____

_____

_____

_____

_____

_____

BEES TO BUTTERFLIES

...Fix your thoughts on what is true, and honorable, and right, and pure, and lovely, and admirable. Think about things that are excellent and worthy of praise.

PHILIPPIANS 4:8

Don't you wish positivity happened more naturally? Why is it so hard for us to consistently keep our minds focused on things that are excellent and praiseworthy?

I don't think of myself as negative by nature. I like laughter and loveliness as much as anybody. I'm also drawn to truth; it tops the list of things I consider important. But honestly, it's a challenge to remain focused on things that are pure, admirable, and true when all things unpleasant and contrary in our busy world seem to constantly vie for my attention. Social media, the news, relationship issues, professional struggles —they all have the potential to affect my peace. Can you relate?

But there's a problem with paying unnecessary attention to the things that tempt, discourage, and defeat us. You see, whatever we think about has a tendency to become what we say and do. If you and I are to experience the joy, peace, patience, and contentment that God wants us to have, we need to replace negative or disheartening thoughts with the praise-worthy thoughts God wants.

A very precious girl in my life says it this way: "In with the butterflies and out with the bees!" This week I want you to practice focusing on the good things God pours into your life. I want you to think about the truth of His grace, mercy, and love. I want you to fill your heart and mind with good news! I want you to replace the bees with butterflies and celebrate God's blessings. What do you say? Are you in?

Start a list of blessings here and copy it into a journal where you can add to it every day this week (and beyond).

_____

_____

_____

_____

_____

_____

Make a list of "the bees"—things you read, watch, listen to, or talk about that tempt, discourage, and frustrate you. Why do you think you keep returning to these things?

_____

_____

_____

_____

_____

_____

Make a list of "the butterflies"—things you read, watch, listen to, and talk about that help you focus on what is true, honorable, pure, lovely, and admirable.

_____

_____

_____

_____

_____

_____

Consider the items from each of your lists and write a prayer of gratitude to God for your blessings. Ask Him to help you consistently focus your thoughts on all things excellent and praiseworthy.

_____

_____

_____

_____

_____

_____

_____

_____

_____

THE BATTLE IS REAL, BUT THE VICTORY IS WON

Don't be afraid, for I am with you.
Don't be discouraged, for I am your God.
I will strengthen you and help you. I will hold
you up with my victorious right hand.
ISAIAH 41:10

The Bible calls the one who has been tempting and taunting God's children since the Garden of Eden the "great enemy." And I don't know about you, but sometimes it seems like that enemy is working overtime in my head to keep me discouraged and disappointed. He taunts me with messages that appear as negative self-talk, like:

I've failed—again!

I'm always messing up.
There's no way God can use me.

The world is terrifying.
I need to hide in fear.

People will always let me down.
I can't count on anyone.

But although the battle is real, the victory has already been won. Jesus defeated sin and death on the cross, which means you and I can reject the discouraging lies told by the great enemy of our souls. How? By focusing on God's promises to be with us, to strengthen us, to help us, and to hold us up with His victorious hand. You and I have everything we need through the One who won the war so we can have victory in the battle.

And just in case you forget for a moment, He also calls you His child, chosen, blessed, treasured, a masterpiece, protected, held, and loved. When you hear the voice of disappointment and discouragement, remember: God loves you, He's with you, and He's made it possible for victory to be yours.

How are you struggling with disappointment and discouragement right now?

_____

_____

_____

Look up John 1:12, John 15:15, and 1 John 3:1, and copy one here. How do the words of those Scriptures make you feel? What are your favorites among the names God calls you?

_____

_____

_____

_____

Meditate upon today's verse, Isaiah 41:10. Does this promise calm your fears and give you courage? Why or why not?

_____

_____

_____

_____

_____

_____

_____

Write a prayer about the things currently discouraging you, asking for God's help to reject the enemy's lies. Surrender your discouragement to Him and thank Him for giving you hope.

_____

_____

_____

_____

_____

_____

_____

LOVABLE

And may you have the power to understand . . .
how wide, how long, how high, and how deep
his love is. May you experience the love of
Christ, though it is too great to understand fully.
Then you will be made complete with all the fullness
of life and power that comes from God.

EPHESIANS 3:18–19

Do you ever have days when you don't feel very lovable?
Please tell me I'm not the only one who feels this way, that
you have days when you wake up fully aware of every one
of your little flaws and faults—physical, emotional, mental,
and spiritual. (I can still remember how frustrated I was the
day I realized it was possible to have zits and wrinkles at
the same time!) You may be able to relate to struggling with
absent-mindedness, procrastination, or occasional bad
attitudes, too. And then there's also that unpleasant problem
you and I can have when people just won't see things the right
way—our way!

Okay, you get the idea.

Unfortunately, when you and I are focused on ourselves
and let things make us feel unlovable, we can start to doubt
God's love for us and pull away from Him. But our insecure,
wobbly moments are the times we really need to embrace the
truth of God's perfect unfailing love.

God doesn't just love us in our shining moments; His love spans the entirety of our existence. Today's Scripture says that God's love demonstrated in and through Christ is "too great to understand fully." It's immeasurable! And it is absolutely not limited by our feelings, words, or actions. When we hold on to the truth of God's unfailing and unchanging love, well, it's hard to keep believing the lies that try to make us believe we're unlovable.

What are the things that make you feel unlovable?

_____

_____

_____

_____

_____

Make a list of things you do love about the beautiful you God created. Don't be shy—these are gifts from God!

_____

_____

_____

_____

_____

_____

Make a list of things you know to be true about God's perfect unfailing love. How do these truths help you overcome feelings of being unlovable?

_____

_____

_____

_____

_____

_____

_____

Write Psalm 143:8 here. Pray the words of this verse every morning this week. Then surrender your day to God in prayer, asking Him to help you trust Him with your feelings, words, and actions.

_____

_____

_____

_____

_____

_____

_____

_____

HARD-TO-UNDERSTAND PEACE

Then you will experience God's peace, which exceeds anything we can understand. His peace will guard your hearts and minds as you live in Christ Jesus.

PHILIPPIANS 4:7

Have you ever experienced an overwhelming sense of peace when you should have been totally wrecked by fear and worry?

A little more than a dozen years ago, my husband, whom I call "Rev" because he's a preacher, came down with an illness that had some of the same symptoms as congestive heart failure. After more than a year of appointments and tests, the doctors finally determined that he had constrictive pericarditis and needed an operation so difficult and dangerous that it was hard to find a doctor willing to do it.

Then God provided. He not only provided the surgeon, He also provided peace—a peace that we still cannot understand or explain. Sure, we had moments when we were anxious, but most of the time we just did what had to be done and prayed like crazy.

Philippians 4:6-7 says, "Don't worry about anything; instead, pray about everything. Tell God what you need and thank him for all he has done. Then you will experience God's peace." The secret to experiencing God's hard-to-understand peace is not in positive thinking or running from our problems. It's in surrendering every worry and fear to God in prayer, remembering that through Christ Jesus our future is secure. No matter what we're going through, God is in control and He is able to give us the peace we need even when we're facing the most unimaginable circumstances.

Think of someone you've known who has exemplified God's peace while living through challenging times. Journal your observations of how their faith seemed to help them.

_____

_____

_____

_____

_____

Remember a time in the past when God gave you peace that was hard to understand or explain. What happened? How did it make you feel?

_____

_____

_____

_____

_____

_____

Why do you think it can be so hard to give up our struggles to God sometimes?

_____

_____

_____

_____

_____

_____

_____

Write a prayer on the following lines surrendering what you're anxious about and ask Him to once again give you the gift of peace.

_____

_____

_____

_____

_____

_____

_____

_____

_____

MAKING PRAYER SIMPLE

...Pray about everything. Tell God what you need,
and thank him for all he has done.

PHILIPPIANS 4:6

What if we make prayer too complicated? What if prayer is simply supposed to be the conversational part of our relationship with God? What if we should simply talk with Him the same way we'd talk to a loving parent or close friend?

Do you have someone you can't wait to call or text throughout the day? The first person you think of when something happens, good or bad? I believe our Heavenly Father wants to be your Someone. Through Jesus, He opened full access to His throne room, inviting us to come and talk with Him about everything and anything, anytime.

All we have to do, according to today's Scripture, is thank God for all He has done and tell Him what we need. It's that simple!

When we thank God for all He has done in the past, we're more likely to trust Him to help us with whatever we're facing today. And when we tell Him what we need, we surrender that need to His loving care. The Bible calls it the antidote to worry. I think it's also a simple description of prayer.

Jesus said, "Seek the Kingdom of God above all else, and he will give you everything you need" (Luke 12:31). So take your simple prayers to God—your need for forgiveness, healing, help, and wisdom; thank Him for all He has done in the past and trust Him to give you everything you need today.

What are some of the ways you might be making prayer too complicated?

_____

_____

_____

_____

_____

_____

Who is your "someone" to call or text throughout the day? What makes that person special to talk to—are they understanding, sympathetic, supportive?

_____

_____

_____

_____

_____

_____

_____

What makes God special to talk to in prayer? How can you remind yourself to talk to God in prayer, just as you would a trusted friend or loved one?

_____

_____

_____

_____

_____

_____

_____

Make a list of everyday things you'd like to talk with God about in prayer. Talk to God about them and thank Him for being your "Someone."

_____

_____

_____

_____

_____

_____

_____

_____

_____

LOVE GOD 100 PERCENT

Jesus replied, "'You must love the Lord your God with all your heart, all your soul, and all your mind.' This is the first and greatest commandment."

MATTHEW 22:37–38

This week's Scripture is quoted often, but have you ever wondered what it really means to love God with all your heart, soul, mind, and strength?

I think most of us get the idea that we're supposed to love Him 100 percent, completely, with all we are and all we have. But I want to know the specifics because Jesus didn't make it optional. He said, "You must," and that's a command.

So let's take a closer look.

Loving God with all your heart *is making your relationship with Him your most precious treasure, valuing it over everything else. Jesus said, "Wherever your treasure is, there the desires of your heart will also be"* *(Luke 12:34).*

Loving God with all your soul *is loving God with all you are—your will, attitude, thoughts, feelings, and health. "Let all that I am praise the Lord; with my whole heart, I will praise his holy name" (Psalm 103:1).*

Loving God with all your mind *is loving Him with your knowledge and understanding. It is taking the time to "be still and know" Him (Psalm 46:10) by spending time in the Word and in prayer. "We destroy arguments and every lofty opinion raised against the knowledge of God, and take every thought captive to obey Christ" (2 Corinthians 10:5, ESV).*

Loving God with all your strength *is putting your love for Him into everything you do and say, using the abilities and blessings He has given you to love others for His glory. . . "Whatever you do, do it all for the glory of God" (1 Corinthians 10:31).*

Although you and I cannot and will not love God the way Jesus commands on our own, with His Spirit's help, we can make loving God 100 percent our life's purpose and our greatest desire.

What gets in the way of you loving God the way Jesus commands? What people, things, teachings, or attitudes make it hard for you to put God first in your life?

_____

_____

_____

_____

_____

_____

_____

Do you find it most difficult to love God with your thoughts, words, actions, or resources? Why?

_____

_____

_____

_____

_____

In what areas of your life do you need God's help to use your abilities to bless and love others for His glory?

_____

_____

_____

_____

_____

Pour your heart out in a prayer to God in the following lines. Honestly share the parts of your life you struggle to surrender and ask for help to make loving Him your heart's desire.

_____

_____

_____

_____

_____

LOVE OTHERS, LOVE YOURSELF

A second [commandment] is equally important:
"Love your neighbor as yourself."
MATTHEW 22:39

If Jesus says loving ourselves and others is important, we should know how to do it. I think we can look at the whole "love yourself"/"love your neighbor" thing in a way that makes doing it simpler.

Jesus's commandment to love others requires you to love yourself as well. So let's start with three things I believe are essential to loving yourself:

1. **Know yourself.** Take the time to think about and learn who God created you to be—your beliefs, personality, talents, gifts, abilities, hopes, and dreams.

2. **Accept yourself.** Refuse to compare yourself to anyone else. Keep your focus on the Lord and strive to be the best version possible of yourself.

3. **Be yourself.** Surrender yourself to God, the One who created you. Allow Him to use you for His plans and purposes.

Yes, self-love depends on fully giving ourselves to God, the One who loves us so much that He created us individually, uniquely, and specifically for this time and place.

But what about loving others? Maybe it's simpler than we think. If we're able to love ourselves, it should be easier to share that same love with others. Maybe loving our neighbors as we love ourselves simply means getting to know them as God created them, accepting them without comparisons or judgment, and encouraging them to be themselves, because they, too, are God's marvelous workmanship!

And in all honesty, isn't that how we want our neighbors to love us?

What do you think about the three components of self-love proposed in this week's devotion? What would you add to or subtract from it?

How well would you say you love yourself? Know yourself? Accept yourself?

_____

_____

_____

_____

_____

How can you do a better job of being yourself, allowing God to use you for His plans and purposes?

_____

_____

_____

_____

Write a prayer honestly telling God about your struggle to love yourself and others the way He commands. Ask Him to help you in this area.

_____

_____

_____

_____

_____

THE GOD WHO SEES YOU

She gave this name to the Lord who spoke to her:
"You are the God who sees me," for she said, "I have
now seen the One who sees me."

GENESIS 16:13 (NIV)

Do you ever have days when your best efforts aren't appreciated? When if you're honest, you'd really like to run away and hide?

Meet Hagar, Sarah's servant. Sarah wanted a baby, and she was tired of waiting, so she decided to make Hagar her surrogate. But as soon as Hagar became pregnant, Sarah grew angry with her husband, Abraham, and jealous of Hagar. Frustrated, she took out her resentment on Hagar.

Can you imagine? You're serving your mistress by growing the baby she wanted. (It certainly wasn't your idea.) Now she's taking her bad attitude out on you in a way the Bible describes as "harsh" or "mistreatment." Hagar took as much as she could . . . and then she ran away into the desert.

I love that when Hagar was in the desert the Lord asked her a simple question: "Where have you come from and where are you going?" God didn't need to hear the answer; Hagar needed to hear the question.

Once she admitted she was running away, God told her to go back and face the future He had already prepared for her.

And she realized that whatever she was going through, wherever she was, God knew. He was the God who saw her.

He sees you, too. He knows what you're going through. He has a future prepared for you. And He is always with you. You can do this! He promises to give you all the help and grace you need (2 Corinthians 12:9).

Have you ever felt caught in a seemingly impossible situation like Hagar? What happened? How did God help you?

_____

_____

_____

_____

_____

Was there a time when you realized you were running away from God and He let you know He saw you? Write about it here.

_____

_____

_____

_____

_____

_____

_____

How does it make you feel to know God sees you and knows what you're going through? Do you ever have trouble believing this? If so, why do you think that is?

_____

_____

_____

_____

_____

_____

_____

Write a prayer telling God how it feels to know He is the One who sees you, even when you are frustrated and discouraged. Ask Him to help you trust the future He has prepared for you.

_____

_____

_____

_____

_____

_____

_____

GOD IS STILL WORKING

And I am certain that God, who began the good work within you, will continue his work until it is finally finished on the day when Christ Jesus returns.

PHILIPPIANS 1:6

I'm a firstborn, a people pleaser, and a perfectionist. Maybe you can relate. Many followers of Jesus struggle with a powerful need to be do-it-right rule followers.

Now, I firmly believe the desire to obey God's commands is a good thing. In fact, I believe it's inspired by the Holy Spirit. But there are several problems with trying to be perfect: It's self-focused, it's impossible, it leaves you feeling incomplete and discouraged, it keeps you from celebrating God's gift of forgiveness with joy, and it makes you less patient with others.

No matter how hard you and I try, we're not perfect, and we won't be this side of heaven. But the good news is God knows that, loves us, and is still working on us.

If you have kids, you know they're not perfect, but you love and forgive them anyway. And even though you don't do it perfectly, you do your best to teach them what's right because you want what's best for them and you don't want them to experience the natural consequences of their mistakes and failures.

In a similar way, God, our perfect Father, loves, forgives, and continually works within us. He made a way for us to be saved through Jesus's death on the cross. And He is making

His saving grace real in us through faith and the power of His Spirit.

You don't have to be perfect. Your Father loves you, and He's still working on you!

List some areas in which you have struggled with trying to be perfect or felt inadequate.

_____

_____

_____

_____

_____

_____

Write all the reasons why you want to be easier on yourself and better trust God to help you become the person you're meant to be.

_____

_____

_____

_____

_____

_____

_____

_____

Make a list of the ways God is a perfect Father to you.

_____

_____

_____

_____

_____

_____

_____

Write a prayer listing a couple of imperfections you'd like to improve upon and ask God for His forgiveness and help. Don't forget to thank Him for being a perfect Father!

_____

_____

_____

_____

_____

_____

_____

_____

_____

WHEN WAITING IS HARD

Wait patiently for the Lord. Be brave and courageous.
Yes, wait patiently for the Lord.

PSALM 27:14

I've prayed and I've waited, and I'm guessing you have, too. You may have pleaded with God for a spouse, a child, a restored relationship, a financial breakthrough, or even a miracle. And if you're like me, the longer you had to wait, the more you wondered whether the longing in your heart would ever be satisfied.

Although waiting is part of life, it's true that the greater the desire, the more difficult the wait. Perhaps we question if God cares about us or hears us, if He's fair, or even if He's able. Honestly, sometimes it can be hard to pray, "Thy will be done"!

But that's when you and I need to remember that God is in control, that He's working on us in the wait, and that His timing is always perfect.

Elisabeth Elliot wrote in her book *Passion and Purity*, "I realized that the deepest spiritual lessons are not learned by His letting us have our way in the end, but by His making us wait, bearing with us in love and patience until we are able to honestly pray what He taught His disciples to pray: 'Thy will be done.'"

Patience in waiting means trusting that God's love is greater than our circumstances and that His plan for us is best. The good news is He'll give us the strength and courage we need to withstand the wait through the truth of His promises. Praise God! We don't have to wait alone. God is with us, giving us everything we need to wait patiently, one day at a time.

Are you more patient or impatient? Write about a time when it was really hard to wait and why.

_____

_____

_____

_____

_____

_____

_____

What helps you most when you're tempted to be impatient?

_____

_____

_____

_____

_____

_____

_____

_____

Have you ever looked back and realized God was actually protecting you from something when He made you wait? Write about it here.

_____

_____

_____

_____

_____

_____

_____

Finish the following sentence: *Lord, I surrender the following things to Your timing and care . . .*

_____

_____

_____

_____

_____

_____

_____

_____

_____

LETTING GO

But forget all that—it is nothing compared to what I am going to do. For I am about to do something new. See, I have already begun! Do you not see it? I will make a pathway through the wilderness. I will create rivers in the dry wasteland.

ISAIAH 43:18–19

A familiar scent, a glimpse of a memorable location, or the tune of an old song, and suddenly I'm reliving a moment that happened years ago. Sometimes it's a good memory, like when I recently bought a beautiful gardenia tree and the fragrant blossoms reminded me of my prom night (a night when my mom and dad made a group of dateless girls feel beautiful, special, and loved). However, more often than I'd like, I've also had memories that caused a twinge of pain, reminding me of something that was broken or someone who was missing.

Letting go of past pain is hard, isn't it? I sometimes wonder if it's even possible. But I also think God understands. He knows how our minds work. After all, He created them.

Take a look at the way Isaiah 43:18 is translated in the Amplified Bible: "Do not [earnestly] remember." I think that might be the best, most God-honoring way to deal with our difficult memories. It's not to wipe them from our minds but to de-emphasize them and intentionally replace them with the truth that God is doing "something new" in our lives. Think about how much you've healed already. As this week's Scripture puts it, God is saying to you, "See, I have already begun!"

He's working on you. He's working in your life and on the people you know and love. He's doing something new in you that is helping you heal and move ahead on the pathway He's preparing for you.

What are some of the ways God has helped you move beyond the difficulties of your past?

_____

_____

_____

_____

_____

_____

When you recall all God has done for you, how do you feel? What about when you think of all God will do for you in the future?

_____

_____

_____

_____

_____

_____

_____

What are a few of your favorite memories—blessings you love to "earnestly remember"?

_____

_____

_____

_____

_____

_____

_____

Make note of some difficult memories and surrender them to God in prayer. Thank Him for the "new things" He is doing in your life.

_____

_____

_____

_____

_____

_____

_____

_____

WHEN I CAN'T, GOD CAN

For I can do everything through Christ,
who gives me strength.
PHILIPPIANS 4:13

Have you ever faced a situation and thought, "I can't do this"? I can't face this diagnosis. I can't lose my job. I can't live with this pain. I can't lose my loved one. I can't do this on my own. I can't. I can't. I can't. I used to have a detailed list of things I was sure would be impossible to endure. I believed if certain things happened, people would find me hiding in my room fully unable to function.

No matter how badly you and I want ease and perfection, things that seem impossible to endure do happen. But the good news is they don't have to be beyond our ability to survive and overcome.

I've known countless people who have risen above horrible crises. I saw each of them do one thing that made all the difference: They surrendered their circumstances to God and asked Him to give them the strength they needed to function for His glory, one moment at a time.

I'm one of those people. In an earlier devotion, I told you about Rev's illness and surgery. Well, two months later my mom fell and broke her arm, hip, and neck. After a month in the hospital and rehab, she fell again, hit her head, and died. Six weeks later, our first grandchild was born premature at

24 weeks' gestation weighing 1 pound, 9 ounces. (He's a happy, healthy 12-year-old today.)

I'll admit I did a lot of crying and a lot of crying out to God during that time. But I didn't run and hide in my room, and I didn't stop functioning. I endured with moment-by-moment strength. That's God's all-sufficient grace, His power that "works best in weakness" (2 Corinthians 12:9). It turns "I can't" into "God can." It is God's power to endure "through Christ, who gives me strength."

Are there things you believe you couldn't possibly endure? What are some of them, and why do they scare you?

_____

_____

_____

_____

_____

Remember a time when God gave you the strength you needed to endure something you believed "impossible." Journal your thoughts.

_____

_____

_____

_____

_____

Look up Romans 8:32, 1 Corinthians 10:13, and 2 Corinthians 12:9. Choose one to write out on the following lines. How do these promises give you strength and peace?

_____

_____

_____

_____

_____

_____

_____

Take the "I can't" problem you're currently facing and write a prayer about it. Ask God to help you trust Him moment by moment and give you the strength you need through His all-sufficient grace.

_____

_____

_____

_____

_____

_____

_____

BUT IF YOU SAY SO

"Master," Simon [Peter] replied, "we worked hard all last night and didn't catch a thing. But if you say so, I'll let the nets down again."

LUKE 5:5

Have you ever read a section of Scripture for what must be the hundredth time, but this time, all of a sudden, some words seem twice as big as the others, practically jumping off the page?

The other day, I was reading the Gospels and reached the section where Jesus told Peter, "Now go out where it is deeper, and let down your nets to catch some fish" (Luke 5:4). This must have seemed counterintuitive to Peter. The best fishing happened in the earliest morning hours, not after the sun had heated the water and the fish dove deeper to swim in cooler water. He was tired, too. And on top of that, he was the professional fisherman, not Jesus.

Still, Peter replied: "But if you say so . . ." (5:5). Those were the words that jumped off the page for me. That's trust! And I believe it's the trust you and I can have as we follow our Lord and Savior, Jesus.

We can say with faith, "But if You say so, I will . . .

- **obey Your commands**
- **follow where You lead**

- forgive when I don't want to
- be patient even when it's hard
- trust Your promises
- believe You call me forgiven, beautiful, child, friend, strong, courageous, and loved
- rely on You to give me hope, patience, and everything I need to endure whatever You allow
- remember You are with me—always!"

You and I can trust the One whose love never fails. We can know that if God says so, He will give us what we need.

Is there any part of your life where you feel overwhelmed and exhausted right now? Write about it here.

_____

_____

_____

_____

_____

How do you struggle with doubt?

_____

_____

_____

_____

When have you been blessed because you simply trusted
and followed God's will?

_____

_____

_____

_____

_____

_____

_____

Write the sentence "But if You say so, I will _____,"
filling in the blank with something you need to surrender to
God. List a few examples and pray over them.

_____

_____

_____

_____

_____

_____

_____

_____

_____

AVOIDING THE COMPARISON TRAP

Pay careful attention to your own work, for then you will get the satisfaction of a job well done, and you won't need to compare yourself to anyone else.

GALATIANS 6:4

Well, I did it again. It wasn't what I intended. In fact, I told myself I'd stop. But then I started scrolling through social media, and before I was even aware of it, I'd fallen for the comparison trap.

Why? Because photos and descriptions of perfectly happy families, wonderful jobs, exciting trips, and skin that looks 20 years younger than mine brought all my feelings of insecurity and discontentment to the surface again.

It's hard, isn't it? It's hard to be humbly satisfied with who we are, what we have, and what we've done. There always seems to be a little part of us that feels like we're lacking. We feel like we don't do enough, make enough, have enough—we simply feel like we're not enough.

But God's Word says that you and I are marvelously made (Psalm 139:14), that we were created with specific God-given gifts and abilities (1 Peter 4:10) to do good works in Jesus's name (Ephesians 2:10), and that through Him we can achieve what He has planned for us.

We are each uniquely made for God's specific plans and purposes. He did not equip us to live our friends' lives, and He didn't equip them to live ours. It's easy to compare someone else's best with our worst, but we have not been given what we need to live their best—or their worst. We've been given what we need to live ours, with God's help, for His glory.

What are some of the things that draw you into the comparison trap?

_____

_____

_____

_____

_____

_____

What can you do this week to celebrate who you are and avoid falling into the comparison trap?

_____

_____

_____

_____

_____

_____

_____

How can you encourage yourself, your family, and your friends to celebrate all of the beautifully unique ways each of you has been created?

_____

_____

_____

_____

_____

Make a list of things you love about yourself and your life. Ask God to help you focus on your blessings, thanking Him for creating you specifically for your one-of-a-kind beautiful life.

_____

_____

_____

_____

_____

_____

_____

_____

_____

_____

WEEK 17

LOVE LIKE JESUS

. . . I am giving you a new commandment:
Love each other. Just as I have loved you,
you should love each other.
JOHN 13:34

How would you rate yourself when it comes to loving
like Jesus, even in times when others don't seem so lovable?
It's hard, isn't it? It takes a lot of effort to love people
when they're being demanding, confrontational, offensive,
or irritating.

I think the problem is that we tend to think of Jesus's
command to love as a command to have warm and fuzzy
feelings for everyone. But the love Jesus asks of us is one that
demonstrates itself in action. Jesus showed us how to love . . .

- **compassionately (Matthew 14:14)**

- **sacrificially (John 15:13)**

- **with humility, patience, kindness, and forgiveness
  (Ephesians 4:2)**

- **without favoritism or prejudice (James 2:8–9)**

- **unconditionally (Colossians 3:14)**

- **even our enemies (Matthew 5:44)**

And that's hard—no, it's impossible! We can't do it on our own. But the good news is we don't have to because we can do everything through Christ, who gives us strength (Philippians 4:13). When loving feels impossible, you and I can go to Jesus and ask Him to give us what we need to show people His love.

We can ask Him to help us look beyond the surface and see in every person someone who is dearly loved and precious to Him. Loving like Jesus is asking Him to help us get out of the way so He can love people through us, to show the world who He is and why we love Him.

Recount when God gave you the strength to love someone else when they were demanding, confrontational, offensive, or irritating.

_____

_____

_____

_____

_____

When has someone loved you when you were hard to love?

_____

_____

_____

_____

_____

Think of someone you see regularly who is hard to love. How can you let Jesus love them through you?

_____

_____

_____

_____

_____

_____

_____

_____

Write a thank-you note to God. Thank Him for loving you even when you're hard to love and pray He'll help you love like Jesus.

_____

_____

_____

_____

_____

_____

_____

THE HELPER

Give all your worries and cares to God,
for he cares about you.
1 PETER 5:7

Everyone is going through something, whether it's a major life change, grief, loneliness, anxiety, stress, illness, chronic pain, or something else.

No matter which issues from that list are true for you, this week I want you to know something really important: God not only cares about your salvation, He also cares about what you're going through in the present. He sent Jesus to live, die, and rise again so that you can experience eternity with Him—but He also gave you the Holy Spirit to give you what you need every day.

In John 14:26, Jesus called the Holy Spirit the Helper: "This Helper is the Holy Spirit whom the Father will send in my name" (NCV). He is with you to help you when you are discouraged, disappointed, overwhelmed, anxious, stressed, lonely, or grieving. He is with you to give you faith, hope, peace, patience, wisdom, and strength. He even prays for you, according to Romans 8:26: "But the Spirit Himself speaks to God for us, even begs God for us with deep feelings that words cannot explain" (NCV).

So whatever you're going through, whatever is hurting your heart or making you anxious, stop this week and give it to

God, trusting that He cares about you and what you're facing. He is with you, praying for you and giving you everything you need.

Remember a time when the Holy Spirit increased your faith and gave you hope, peace, patience, wisdom, or strength when you needed it. What happened? How did it make you feel?

_____

_____

_____

_____

_____

What are you worried about this week? Write down everything you can think of, big and small.

_____

_____

_____

_____

_____

_____

_____

Now identify your top two or three worries from the list and write them here. Then take a marker or colored pencil in a bright, beautiful color and write "GOD CARES" over the top of the words.

_____

_____

_____

_____

_____

_____

_____

Write a prayer thanking God for caring about you and your concerns and for giving you the Holy Spirit to help you.

_____

_____

_____

_____

_____

_____

_____

_____

BE STILL

God says, "Be still and know that I am God. I will be
praised in all the nations; I will be praised throughout
the earth." The Lord All-Powerful is with us; the God
of Jacob is our defender.
PSALM 46:10–11 (NCV)

Those words—"be still"—get me every time. They always
remind me of my parents and teachers shushing me for talking
too much. Nowadays, I can do a somewhat better job of
keeping my thoughts to myself, but finding stillness of mind is
harder. Even if I'm not saying it aloud, there's just so much to
think about, isn't there?

But maybe that's not the point.

Maybe God is making a different point about stillness:
"Get yourself and your thoughts out of the way and think
about Me." A common biblical name for God is Yahweh
(often anglicized as Jehovah), which roughly translates from
Hebrew as "I AM" (see Exodus 3:14). Maybe when God tells
us to be still, He's saying, "Focus less on your own identity
and remember that I am God! Remember that I am Creator,
Redeemer, Helper, Father, and Friend. I am Almighty, Eternal,
All-Powerful, Defender, and Unfailing Love. I've got this!"

What else does Psalm 46 say? God will help you in times
of trouble (46:1). You don't need to be afraid (46:2). For these
reasons, you and I can be still! We can quietly pause, getting

ourselves out of the way, and know God. When we do, nothing in this world can shake our foundation because "the Lord All-Powerful is with us. The God of Jacob is our Defender."

This week, be still and know that God, the Great "I AM," is with you. You have nothing to worry about.

Does an overactive mind, a hectic schedule, or something else make it hard for you to "be still" with God? How so?

_____

_____

_____

_____

_____

Choose one or two of the following verses that will help you know God: Isaiah 40:28, Psalm 18:30, John 14:6, Romans 5:8, 1 John 4:10, Matthew 28:20. Write them here. Then find 10 or 15 spare minutes when you can sit quietly and meditate on them this week.

_____

_____

_____

_____

_____

What does it mean to you that God called Himself "I AM"? What characteristics of God does it highlight?

_____

_____

_____

_____

_____

_____

_____

_____

Write a prayer asking God to help you calm your mind and your schedule so you can "be still" and know Him the way He wants you to know Him, trust Him, and follow Him.

_____

_____

_____

_____

_____

_____

_____

YOU ARE LOVED

And I am convinced that nothing can ever separate us from God's love . . . No power in the sky above or in the earth below—indeed, nothing in all creation will ever be able to separate us from the love of God that is revealed in Christ Jesus our Lord.

ROMANS 8:38–39

I was driving across the Jefferson Barracks Bridge, south of St. Louis, on my way to speak at a women's retreat in Belleville, Illinois. I was singing along with some of my favorite worship songs when the Holy Spirit prompted me to turn off my music so I could simply pray and listen.

I quieted my heart and mind and said, "Father, I'm prepared to speak to these ladies about the ways You've been working in my life, but is there something specific You'd like them to know?"

And I sensed His reply: "Tell them I love them!"

Doubting it would be that simple, I said, "Father, I'm sure they know You love them. Are You sure there isn't anything else You want them to know?"

And I felt Him say, "Yes, they know. But someone in that room needs to hear you say it today."

So that's what I did. Toward the end of my morning presentation, I told those women about the conversation I'd had with God on the drive over that morning. And during our lunch break, a reticent attendee hesitantly approached me and told me about the difficult problems she was facing. She said that she had been so overwhelmed that she'd started doubting God's love. And then she said, "I know God's message of love was meant for me! I'm the one who needed to hear it!"

That's how personally loving and caring He is! God loves each of us as if there were only one of us. And nothing in all creation can remove us from His love.

How do you feel when you are reminded that God loves you?

_____

_____

_____

_____

_____

Do you know someone who needs to hear God say, "I love you"? Write their name(s) here. How might you express God's love to them?

_____

_____

_____

_____

_____

_____

_____

Read 1 John 4:9–10 and imagine what God would say if He wrote a love letter to you personally. Write it here.

_____

_____

_____

_____

_____

_____

_____

Write a prayer as your reply to the love letter from God you wrote in the previous section. Tell Him what it means to you that He wants you to know how very much He loves you.

_____

_____

_____

_____

_____

_____

_____

_____

WHEN YOU WONDER WHAT TO DO

Trust in the Lord with all your heart; do not depend on your own understanding. Seek his will in all you do, and he will show you which path to take.

PROVERBS 3:5–6

Do you ever wonder if you are following God's will for your life? Do you lie awake at night questioning whether you're heading in the right direction? Do you wish God would supernaturally hand you a prewritten to-do list to help you know you're doing things His way?

For me the answer is yes, all of the above!

Decision making is a big part of life, and it's stressful no matter how we look at it. Where should we live? Are we on the right career path? How many children should we have? Should we homeschool? Is this healthy? Am I doing enough? Am I doing too much? And on and on and on. But there are a few things you and I can do when we're faced with a difficult decision.

1. **Ask God.** Pray and ask Him to help you make this decision according to His plans and purposes for you.

2. **Ask yourself.** Will this decision glorify God? Will it bless my family (not just financially but relationally and

emotionally)? Will it interfere with my ability to love God and others?

3. **Wait.** Be patient and willing to wait on God's timing.

4. **Trust God.** Be certain that if He wants something specific in your life, He'll make it clear to you.

Then get up each day and live your life. You can have peace knowing that if your desire is to trust and glorify God with your life, He will show you what to do.

Write about a time God used circumstances or other people to help you make a decision.

_____

_____

_____

_____

_____

When has it been hardest to wait on God while you were wondering what to do?

_____

_____

_____

_____

_____

_____

Think of a decision you need to make and ask yourself if it will glorify God, bless your family, or interfere with your ability to love. Journal your thoughts.

_____

_____

_____

_____

_____

_____

_____

Think about a decision you're trying to make right now. Write a prayer asking God to guide you according to His loving plans and purposes. Thank Him for caring about you and the decisions you make.

_____

_____

_____

_____

_____

_____

_____

_____

HOW I PROTECTED YOU

The Lord keeps watch over you as you come and go,
both now and forever.

PSALM 121:8

I was having one of those days. Painful memories had me mentally reliving the past and aching for what was missing in the present. So, as I'd done countless times before, I cried out to God.

In that moment, I didn't sense His impatience or disapproval. Instead, my heart heard Him gently whisper, "You have no idea how I've protected you."

One short perspective-changing sentence.

I'd been so focused on what I was missing, I hadn't even considered that God might have been using this broken situation to protect me from far worse possibilities. Suddenly, by His grace and gentle prompting, my focus turned from me to Him. I realized that the Lord had been carefully watching over me the whole time.

It's kind of funny, isn't it? You and I have these plans. We think we know how things are supposed to go. We want what we want, and we want God to get on board and help things go our way.

But what we can too often forget is that He knows the future before it even happens. He knows what's best for us, and nothing will keep Him from lovingly watching over us.

Whatever your circumstances, whatever is lost or lacking, your Heavenly Father knows and cares. He is watching over you and He wants you to know: "You have no idea how I've protected you."

What painful memories most often rob your joy and tank your mood?

_____

_____

_____

_____

_____

_____

In what ways might God have been protecting you as you were going through something painful?

_____

_____

_____

_____

_____

_____

_____

How does it feel to consider that God knows your future before it happens and that your current problems might be His way of protecting you? Write your feelings here.

_____

_____

_____

_____

_____

_____

Write a prayer thanking God for protecting you even when you weren't aware. Ask Him to help you remember how much He loves you and watches over you even when painful memories or current problems seem overwhelming.

_____

_____

_____

_____

_____

_____

_____

_____

UN-BRUTAL HONESTY

An honest witness tells the truth; a false witness tells lies. Some people make cutting remarks, but the words of the wise bring healing.

PROVERBS 12:17–18

There's a common two-word phrase that sets my nerves on edge and prevents me from truly hearing anything that is said subsequently. What is it? "Brutal honesty!"

I am 100 percent for truth and honesty, but I have never understood the need to express it brutally. I understand that when someone uses this phrase, they're disclosing that they understand what they're about to say may not be well received. But to be brutal is to be harsh, cruel, or insensitive. Can "brutal honesty" ever truly offer God's healing love?

How can you and I be honest the way God wants us to be honest? To answer that question, let's look at God's Word.

Jesus said, "Make them holy by your truth; teach them your word, which is truth" (John 17:17). And Peter wrote, "If someone asks about your hope as a believer, always be ready to explain it. But do this in a gentle and respectful way" (1 Peter 3:15–16).

Those verses reveal how you and I can be honest, God's way. First, know the truth of God's Word, and then talk to everyone in a way that represents God's love, being both gentle and respectful.

I'll be the first to admit that it's not easy to consistently use wise words that bring healing, but with God's help we can try. Whether we're having a difficult conversation or sharing the truth of God's Word, we can be the people who replace brutal honesty with grace-filled truth that heals. Are you in?

How do you feel about the phrase "brutal honesty"? Would you describe yourself as brutally honest?

_____

_____

_____

_____

_____

_____

Write about a time someone was brutally honest with you. Did it make it easier or harder to hear the truth? To feel God's love?

_____

_____

_____

_____

_____

_____

_____

How has God's love changed your life? Write about how you can represent God's love to someone (a child, a spouse, a friend, or even an enemy) by speaking with gentleness and respect.

_____

_____

_____

_____

_____

_____

Think about a difficult conversation you need to have. Write a prayer asking God to help you represent His love by wisely speaking gently and respectfully. Ask Him to help you bring healing to the person and to the relationship.

_____

_____

_____

_____

_____

_____

_____

SAFE FRIENDS

Don't just pretend to love others. Really love them. Hate what is wrong. Hold tightly to what is good. Love each other with genuine affection, and take delight in honoring each other.

ROMANS 12:9–10

Although it was several years ago, I can still picture where each of us sat at the table. We'd only met in person 24 hours earlier. I'll admit, I was nervous wondering how we'd all get along. We were all women and bloggers, but we spanned four decades in age (I was the oldest), we came from seven different states and the British Virgin Islands, and though we didn't discuss politics, we probably had different political views.

But then someone asked, "What's your testimony? I don't want to just know about you. I want to know you!"

And over the next several hours, we went around the table telling each other about the broken parts of our lives and the beautiful ways Jesus had delivered and healed us.

I will never forget how safe I felt that night as God's love poured over us and through us. We listened to each other without judgment. We offered each other kindness and compassion.

It's a gift from God to feel safe enough with others to trust them with the imperfect parts of our stories. And if it is a gift we want to give, we need to promise that their testimony is not ours to tell. We need to promise to pray for them, not talk about them. Keeping these promises makes us a safe friend.

We all want and need safe friends, people with whom we can be our true selves. And with God's help, we can be safe friends who know, pray for, and love each other.

In your opinion, what are the most important attributes of a safe friend?

_____

_____

_____

_____

_____

_____

Make a list of people you consider safe friends. How do you treasure these friends?

_____

_____

_____

_____

_____

_____

_____

_____

How can you share the ways Jesus has delivered you and
healed the broken parts of your story?

_____

_____

_____

_____

_____

_____

_____

_____

Thank God for your safe friends and write something specific you can pray about for each of them right now. Ask
God to help you consistently show them compassion and
kindness.

_____

_____

_____

_____

_____

_____

_____

LIVE GUILT-FREE

*...For our guilty consciences have been sprinkled
with Christ's blood to make us clean, and our bodies
have been washed with pure water. Let us hold tightly
without wavering to the hope we affirm, for God can
be trusted to keep his promise.*

HEBREWS 10:22–23

I'm an expert at feeling guilt. I can dredge up guilty feelings
over choices I made decades ago. I've questioned thousands of
times how I could have done things differently or how I could
have altered events to reshape the outcome.

But there's a problem with carrying old guilt: It becomes
a burden that makes it impossible to fully enjoy the freedom
we have in and through Jesus's death and resurrection. Guilt
holds us captive to a lie—a lie that says Jesus's sacrifice
wasn't enough, that you and I have to do something in addition
to what He has already done for us.

But that's not what Jesus said. Jesus said . . .

*"There is joy in the presence of God's angels when even
one sinner repents." (Luke 15:10)*

*"There is forgiveness of sins for all who repent."
(Luke 24:47)*

"If the Son sets you free, you are truly free." (John 8:36)

The freedom Jesus gives us means we don't have to carry our guilt around for another moment. His freedom makes it possible for you and me to truly become the people we were created to be. Jesus's freedom gives us the strength we need to fight temptation. Jesus's freedom removes our guilt and gives us hope, peace, and joy. I think it's time to give our guilt to God and celebrate the blessing of forgiveness and freedom we have in Jesus. Freedom to live. Freedom to love. Freedom to thrive, guilt-free!

Are you an expert at feeling guilty? How often do you struggle with the past?

How does it make you feel to know Jesus took your guilt to the cross? (If it makes you feel guiltier, pray about it!)

Write about a past experience that's hard to let go of. Why is it difficult to surrender it to God, once and for all?

_____

_____

_____

_____

_____

_____

_____

Write a prayer asking God to help you receive the freedom from guilt that He has promised you and to give you faith to know that you are forgiven and free in Christ.

_____

_____

_____

_____

_____

_____

_____

_____

CREATING BALANCE

You will show me the way of life,
granting me the joy of your presence and the
pleasures of living with you forever.
PSALM 16:11

This year was going to be different. You started it with res-
olutions and goals, a list of things you were going to change
to have the life balance God wants for you . . . but then you
brought last year's schedule, people, and expectations into
this year's lifestyle. Now you're stuck in your old exhausting
routine.

Slowing down isn't easy, but it's necessary if you want
to live peacefully and according to your priorities. If you're
struggling, here are some ways to start creating life balance.

1. **Assess your to-do list and calendar to see where you
   spend the most time.** Prioritize your schedule by labeling
   nonnegotiable obligations as "Have To," things that are necessary to accomplish your goals as "Need To," and things
   you do for pleasure as "Want To."

2. **Look for things you can remove from your schedule.**
   Identify and get rid of anything that isn't the best use of
   your time, talents, and treasures.

3. **Set boundaries.** It's perfectly okay to say no to people.

4. **Ask for help.** Remember, you may be denying someone else the opportunity to use their gifts and abilities when you try to be and do everything for everyone.

Finally, surrender your schedule and to-do list to God. Ask Him to give you wisdom, help, and strength to create the balance you want and that you know He wants for you. God has plans and purposes for you, and it pleases Him when you surrender your life and your schedule to Him.

List 10 or so of your gifts, abilities, and skills.

_____

_____

_____

_____

_____

Look at your planner. Write down which gifts and skills you'll use in upcoming plans or events.

_____

_____

_____

_____

_____

_____

_____

Are the plans and events on your calendar making the best use of your time and abilities? List the things that someone else might be able to help you accomplish.

_____

_____

_____

_____

_____

_____

_____

Write a prayer incorporating two or three gifts from the preceding list, asking God to use them for His glory while also helping you find balance and peace.

_____

_____

_____

_____

_____

_____

_____

_____

PEACE IN THE PAIN

You will keep in perfect peace all who trust in you,
all whose thoughts are fixed on you!
ISAIAH 26:3

It's often said that something cannot be morally wrong as long as no one gets hurt. But anytime a person goes against God's will, that person hurts themselves and anyone involved. Everyone touched by the wrong, even those on the perimeter, have their peace, contentment, and joy confronted.

I think that's where focusing on and trusting in the Lord changes everything. Jesus said that God's will for us is love—loving the Lord and loving others (Matthew 22:37). Peter wrote, "Most important of all, continue to show deep love for each other, for love covers a multitude of sins" (1 Peter 4:8).

Jesus also said that we are to be people who forgive (Luke 6:37). And Paul added, "Be kind to each other, tenderhearted, forgiving one another, just as God through Christ has forgiven you" (Ephesians 4:32).

When you and I fix our thoughts, hearts, and minds on the Lord, when we know His will and do our best to carefully follow it, we love better. And that includes forgiving ourselves and the people who cause us pain. And forgiveness is what gives us the perfect peace that we want and that God wants for us.

If we want to enjoy peace in the midst of chaos and pain, we have to remember: No matter who or what is the source of our suffering, love and forgiveness are the things that bring healing peace to the story of those who trust in and focus on Jesus.

When has someone else hurt you by saying or doing something they believed was fine because "no one would get hurt"?

_____

_____

_____

_____

_____

_____

When have you hurt someone else with the same sort of words or actions?

_____

_____

_____

_____

_____

_____

How has God's love and forgiveness made a difference in your life in either or both of these situations?

_____

_____

_____

_____

_____

_____

Write a prayer asking God to forgive you for the times you unintentionally hurt someone and to help you forgive those who hurt you. Then thank Him for the blessing of His healing peace through forgiveness.

_____

_____

_____

_____

_____

_____

_____

BE HUMBLE, GENTLE, AND PATIENT

Always be humble and gentle. Be patient with each other, making allowance for each other's faults because of your love.

EPHESIANS 4:2

If you're like me, you may have read the title and verse at the top of this devotion and thought about just turning the page and moving on. I understand! If there's anything that makes me squirm, it's realizing how far away from "always" I am when it comes to humility, gentleness, and patience.

I come up with excuses. I want to believe that when the apostle Paul wrote these words, he didn't mean I should be humble, gentle, and patient even when I'm driving, or when the kids are making me crazy, or when I'm in the middle of an argument and someone hurts my feelings. He couldn't have meant "always" in those situations, could he?

Like it or not, I think he did.

You and I want and need others to be humble, gentle, patient, and quick to forgive us, so we need to be humble, gentle, patient, and quick to forgive them. More specifically, Jesus said, "Here is a simple rule of thumb for behavior: Ask yourself what you want people to do for you; then grab the initiative and do it for them" (Luke 6:31, MSG).

With God's help, you and I have the power to bless our relationships and demonstrate God's love. I want that! Don't you? So let's stop and pray for those people with whom we disagree, those who have gotten on our last nerve, and those who have hurt our feelings. I believe God is willing and able to give us everything we need to be humble, gentle, patient, and quick to forgive, even when it's hard and we don't want to.

When is it hardest for you to offer gentleness, patience, and forgiveness with humility?

_____

_____

_____

_____

_____

_____

Where is it hardest for you to be gentle, kind, and forgiving (in traffic, at home, at work, at church)? How can you keep yourself from being so affected in these places?

_____

_____

_____

_____

_____

_____

Who are the people you feel the Lord is asking you to pray for?

_____

_____

_____

_____

_____

_____

Write a prayer for those people you may be reluctant to pray for. Ask God to help you be humble and gentle with patience to bless your relationships.

_____

_____

_____

_____

_____

_____

_____

_____

_____

_____

FILLED WITH JOY

*I have told you these things so that you will be filled
with my joy. Yes, your joy will overflow!*
JOHN 15:11

I love reading the Chronological Life Application Study Bible
because it organizes the events of the Bible in the order they
happened rather than the usual book order. This means the
Gospels are grouped together in one sequential account of
Jesus's life and teachings. While reading this version of the
Gospels, I noticed something that made me wonder how often
I've viewed Jesus as a hard-to-please teacher focused on what
I need to improve, and I began to question whether that image
was causing me to miss the real Jesus.

As I read about His miracles and parables, I started to
imagine Jesus's expressions and body language, and God
filled me with this picture of Jesus laughing and smiling. I saw
someone who crowds flocked to because He was happy and
engaging. And many of His words take on a different sentiment
if we imagine Jesus smiling rather than stern.

Just imagine Jesus tenderly smiling as He said . . .

- **"Let the children come to me. Don't stop them!"**
  (Matthew 19:14)
- **"My child, your sins are forgiven." (Mark 2:5)**
- **"Follow me and be my disciple." (Luke 5:27)**

- "Why are you afraid? You have so little faith!" (Matthew 8:26)
- "Why did you doubt me?" (Matthew 14:31)
- "Let's go off by ourselves and rest awhile." (Mark 6:31)

What if some people see Jesus as stern because that's the way you and I represent Him? What if, as in this week's Scripture, they saw His joy overflowing instead? What if we laughed and smiled more? What if we praised what's good more than we criticized what's not? Imagine how we could love others like Jesus if we overflowed with His joy.

How do you picture Jesus when you read the accounts of His teachings and miracles?

_____

_____

_____

_____

Name some of the people you know who overflow with joy because of Jesus's love. How do they show it?

_____

_____

_____

_____

_____

What are your favorite ways to add the joy of Jesus to your life? Look at your planner and add at least one thing every day this week.

_____

_____

_____

_____

_____

_____

_____

Tell God about the ways you picture Him and write a prayer asking Him to help you see Him as He really is.

_____

_____

_____

_____

_____

_____

_____

_____

GOD IS FOR YOU

. . . If God is for us, who can ever be against us?
ROMANS 8:31

Do you know people who make you feel loved, safe, and secure? Do you also know people who don't? I think we all have someone (or several someones) who has been "against us"—people who have betrayed us, lied to us, or otherwise hurt us.

But this week, I want to focus on the truth that no matter how people treat us, we have a Heavenly Father who is, as this week's Scripture says, "for us." No matter who we are or what we've done. No matter how people treat us or what they say about us. No matter how good we try to be or how far we miss the mark of God's will.

God is for us!

How can we know this promise is absolutely true? Romans 8:32 says, "Since he did not spare even his own Son but gave him up for us all, won't he also give us everything else?" If you aren't positively certain without a doubt that God is for you, read those words again. If God gave His Son to die for you, He will not reject you. If Jesus willingly died for you, He wants to spend eternity in heaven with you. If the Lord loves you so much He gave up everything for you, you can be certain He wants to give you everything you need each day to live for His glory.

So if you're feeling less than loved, beautiful, chosen, or precious, I want you to write the words "God is for me" on a sticky note (or several sticky notes), stick it up somewhere in your home, and repeat, "God is for me" until you're confident that it is absolutely 100 percent true!

How have someone's words or actions left you with feelings of insecurity in the past?

_____

_____

_____

_____

_____

_____

When was the last time you questioned whether you were good enough?

_____

_____

_____

_____

_____

_____

_____

_____

Write out Romans 8:31–32, replacing the word *us* with your name (or the word *her*).

_____

_____

_____

_____

_____

_____

_____

What is your greatest insecurity? Write a prayer asking God to help you focus on the truth that no matter how someone treats you, He is always "for you."

_____

_____

_____

_____

_____

_____

_____

_____

_____

WHEN GOD SAYS NO

"For I know the plans I have for you," says the Lord.
"They are plans for good and not for disaster, to give
you a future and a hope."
JEREMIAH 29:11

Your heart is broken. You've prayed and waited, cried and pleaded, but you're still sick, still single, or still longing for a child, a job, a home, or a mended relationship. On top of it all, you look around and countless people seem to have the very thing your heart aches for—and they don't even seem to appreciate it.

We love to quote Jeremiah 29:11, but we rarely look at verse 10, in which the Lord says to the people of Israel, "You will be in Babylon for seventy years." Seventy years of captivity! Why would God allow such a difficult thing to happen? Because He knows that it is in our struggles and pain that we turn to Him and grow. I love the second half of the verse where He adds, "But then I will come and do for you all the good things I have promised, and I will bring you home again."

The good things God promised may not look exactly the way you and I want, but they will be a blessing. I've had times when my response to God's "no" was downright ugly. But I've also learned that anything God allows is always filtered through His love. He will not leave us to suffer alone. He will sustain us and give us everything we need each day. He has a beautiful future planned for each of us.

Jeremiah 29:12–13 says, "In those days when you pray, I will listen. If you look for me wholeheartedly, you will find me." You and I will grow closer to our Father God as we trust His perfect love even when He says no.

When have you had to say no to a child because what they wanted wasn't good for them?

_____

_____

_____

_____

_____

_____

When has God said no to your prayers? How did you handle not getting what you wanted?

_____

_____

_____

_____

_____

_____

_____

What does it mean to you that anything God allows is filtered through His love?

_____

_____

_____

_____

_____

_____

_____

Write a prayer telling God about your current longings and disappointments, and ask Him to help you seek Him and trust with all your heart.

_____

_____

_____

_____

_____

_____

_____

_____

DON'T WORRY

So don't worry about tomorrow, for tomorrow
will bring its own worries. Today's trouble
is enough for today.
MATTHEW 6:34

If worrying were an Olympic sport, I'd have a shelf full of gold medals. I first started worrying when I was a little girl, and it worked so well for me that by the time I was a wife and mom, I had practically perfected my skills. I knew what the Bible said about worrying, and I trusted in Jesus for my eternal well-being, but I didn't trust Him to give me what I needed if any of my what-if scenarios actually happened.

That is, until God allowed me to experience several of the things I had worried about the most—my husband's heart surgery, our first grandchild born prematurely, and more. Then something amazing happened: Through His Word and promises, God gave me the strength I needed to lean on Him and trust His love one moment at a time. He prompted me to pray each time I was tempted to worry.

Are you an anxiety Olympian? Even if you're not, you might have a good reason to be worried right now. You or someone you love may be fighting an illness. Your job may be in jeopardy, and you may be wondering how you're going to pay the bills. You may be emotionally drained trying to help a tantrum-throwing toddler or a rebellious teenager. Or you may feel anxious about a contentious relationship.

The good news is you and I don't have to carry our concerns alone. God wants us to have what we need to endure life's troubles, and He promises to give it to us when we surrender to Him in faith.

What are some of the things you are tempted to worry about most often?

_____

_____

_____

_____

_____

Make a list of things you worried about in the past that never actually happened.

_____

_____

_____

_____

_____

_____

_____

Think about the times God has given you the strength you needed as you experienced life's "trouble."

_____

_____

_____

_____

_____

_____

Make a list of things you're worried about. Then thank God for the times He has given you strength and hope when life was hard. Ask Him to help you surrender your current worries to Him and experience His hard-to-understand peace.

_____

_____

_____

_____

_____

_____

_____

_____

THE PERFECT WOMAN

She is clothed with strength and dignity,
and she laughs without fear of the future.
When she speaks, her words are wise, and
she gives instructions with kindness.
PROVERBS 31:25–26

In Proverbs 31, King Lemuel lists the things his mother taught him about what a truly excellent woman and wife is like. But the queen's advice has put a lot of pressure on the rest of us to live up to those standards! I would love to be the epitome of a Proverbs 31 woman, but the truth is, it's not going to happen. Please tell me you fall short of her perfection, too!

But . . . what if we're supposed to do our best to model her character qualities rather than striving for the impossible goal of being exactly like her? Let's take a closer look at her attributes and at what other verses in Scripture say about how you and I can have them as well.

PROVERBS 31	ALTERNATE VERSE
She *"fears [that is, loves, trusts, and obeys] the Lord"* (Proverbs 31:30).	*"Seek the Kingdom of God above all else"* (Luke 12:31).

PROVERBS 31	ALTERNATE VERSE
"When she speaks, her words are wise" (Proverbs 31:26).	*"If you need wisdom, ask our generous God, and he will give it to you"* (James 1:5).
She is "capable," using her gifts and abilities for good (Proverbs 31:10).	*"God has given each of you a gift from his great variety of spiritual gifts. Use them well to serve one another"* (1 Peter 4:10).
She "opens her arms to the needy" and treats others with kindness (Proverbs 31:20).	*"Since God chose you to be the holy people he loves, you must clothe yourselves with tenderhearted mercy, kindness, humility, gentleness, and patience"* (Colossians 3:12).

The Proverbs 31 woman is who she is because she loves God and wants to glorify Him with her life. Although you and I will never do it perfectly this side of heaven, we can make it the desire of our heart. "Take delight in the Lord, and he will give you your heart's desires" (Psalm 37:4). When we delight in Him, when we seek Him first, when we pursue wisdom and use our gifts for His glory with kindness and compassion, the Lord's will becomes our heart's desire. And those are prayers He loves to answer with a huge "YES!"

Does the Proverbs 31 woman inspire or intimidate you?

How often do you compare yourself to other women?

List your favorite ways to use your gifts and abilities and do a little self-evaluation on how well you treat others with kindness and compassion.

Write down some of the challenges of trying to live with the character qualities of a Proverbs 31 woman. Talk to God about them and honestly ask Him to help you.

THE TRUTH ABOUT WISDOM

*Tune your ears to wisdom, and concentrate
on understanding. Cry out for insight, and
ask for understanding.*

PROVERBS 2:2–3

Who's the wisest person you know? Wisdom isn't just
knowledge. It's knowledge combined with insight and good
judgment. To put it another way, wisdom is knowing the right
thing to do and then doing it. But who decides or defines what
the right thing to do is? The truth is, the only wisdom that
truly protects us from foolishness and its consequences is
God's wisdom! So the question is: How do you and I get God's
wisdom? Here are a few pointers.

1. **Trust God.** "Trust in the Lord with all your heart; do not
   depend on your own understanding. Seek his will in all you
   do, and he will show you which path to take" (Proverbs
   3:5–6). Believe that even when you don't know what to do,
   God knows, and He will guide you if you let Him.

2. **Ask God.** "If you need wisdom, ask our generous God, and
   he will give it to you" (James 1:5). Take your questions and
   uncertainty to Him in prayer. He promises to give you the
   wisdom you need to know His will.

3. **Study the Scriptures.** "You have been taught the holy Scriptures from childhood, and they have given you the wisdom to receive the salvation that comes by trusting in Christ Jesus" (2 Timothy 3:15). The Bible is full of the truth and wisdom—words inspired by the Holy Spirit to guide and bless us.

4. **Do the right thing.** "Fear of the Lord is the foundation of true wisdom. All who obey His commandments will grow in wisdom. Praise Him forever!" (Psalm 111:10) Trusting and obeying God's commands is always the wise thing to do.

Praise God! It's a blessing to know that not only is the Lord willing to help us know the right thing to do—He'll also help us do it!

Who is the wisest person you know? What makes them wise?

_____

_____

_____

_____

How do you decide the right thing to do?

_____

_____

_____

_____

When do you find it hard to do the right thing even when you know what it is?

_____

_____

_____

_____

_____

_____

_____

Are you struggling to act wisely in a specific situation right now? Write a prayer asking God to help you know what to do—and to trust Him enough to actually do it.

_____

_____

_____

_____

_____

_____

_____

_____

YOU ARE PRECIOUS

How precious are your thoughts about me, O God.
They cannot be numbered!
PSALM 139:17

Do you believe this week's Bible verse is true? That God's thoughts about you are precious?

I have to admit, I often have a hard time imagining that God considers me precious. Oh, I believe He loves me. But considers me precious? That's harder to get through my head because I know He is well aware of my thoughts, my motives, my less-than-precious attitudes. Maybe you can relate.

But then I read these words of Jesus in Matthew 13:46: "When he discovered a pearl of great value, he sold everything he owned and bought it!"

You are so precious to God that He gave up the glories of heaven to become like you in every way except for sin. So precious to Him that He died to save you and give you life. So dear to Him that He promises you "hope and a good future" (Jeremiah 29:11, NCV). So beloved to Him that He promises to be "with you always" (Matthew 28:20). And so valuable to Him that He promises to personally come and take you home to heaven (John 14:3).

That's not just love for the whole world. That is the God of the universe declaring you precious. So precious that He gave up everything so He could give you everything.

When you're tempted this week to feel like you're anything less than valued, stop and remember that your Heavenly Father is thinking precious thoughts about you at this very moment.

Write out John 3:16, replacing *the world* with your name.

_____

_____

_____

_____

_____

_____

_____

Look up Ephesians 2:10, Jeremiah 29:11, and Romans 8:32. Choose one to write down and replace the relevant pronouns with your own name.

_____

_____

_____

_____

_____

_____

_____

_____

How does it make you feel to know that God sees you as precious and valuable to Him? Why do you think you feel that way?

_____

_____

_____

_____

_____

_____

_____

Write a prayer thanking God for declaring you precious just the way He made you, even when you struggle to believe it.

_____

_____

_____

_____

_____

_____

_____

_____

_____

BATTLE-READY

Therefore, put on every piece of God's armor so you will be able to resist the enemy in the time of evil. Then after the battle you will still be standing firm.

EPHESIANS 6:13

Are you a battle-ready warrior, prepared for every spiritual attack? I'd like to be. I always believed I would reach a point in my life when I'd anticipate and plan for every inevitable conflict and crisis. Unfortunately, there are still times when I'm surprised and unprepared—typically right after a spiritual high or when life is easy and all is right with the world. You probably have your own vulnerable points.

That's why it's so important for you and me to stay battle-ready. Satan loves to taunt us with lies, so we need to know God's truth. Satan loves to attack our emotions, so we need to focus on God's love and forgiveness. Satan will attack our circumstances and plant seeds of doubt, so we need to fully depend on God to equip us and help us.

The good news is that we can go into battle prepared. We have the covering of God's armor and His weapons with which to fight: "God's Word is an indispensable weapon. In the same way, prayer is essential in this ongoing warfare. Pray hard and long" (Ephesians 6:17–18, MSG).

And remember, Jesus has already won the war! Take a look at John 16:33: "Here on earth you will have many trials and sorrows. But take heart, because I have overcome the world." We don't have to miss out on peace and contentment because we're afraid of the next battle. And we don't have to lose hope in combat. There will be an "after the battle." Seasons come and go, but we never fight alone. God has promised to give us everything we need.

When have you experienced a spiritual attack that caught you by surprise? (Maybe when you were tempted to doubt God's love, struggled with temptation, or lost your hope.)

_____

_____

_____

_____

_____

_____

How can you prepare your heart and mind in advance for the enemy's lies, emotional attacks, or crisis circumstances?

_____

_____

_____

_____

_____

How does it make you feel to know there will always be an "after the battle" because Jesus has already won the war?

_____

_____

_____

_____

_____

_____

_____

How has God helped you through a specific time of temptation or doubt? Write a prayer thanking Him for helping you fight the battle, and ask Him to help you trust Him in the future.

_____

_____

_____

_____

_____

_____

_____

TIME TO DECLUTTER

... since we are surrounded by such a huge crowd of witnesses to the life of faith, let us strip off every weight that slows us down, especially the sin that so easily trips us up. And let us run with endurance the race God has set before us.

HEBREWS 12:1

Have you ever watched *Hoarders*? It's a TV show about people who have reached a point of personal crisis caused by the compulsion to accumulate and hold on to stuff regardless of its purpose or value.

Despite how neat and organized our homes might look, we can easily struggle with a similar clutter that hurts our souls. Things like discontentment, guilt, shame, fear, worry, insecurity, envy, anger, unforgiveness—and the list goes on. Things we never should have held on to, but that we chose to store just in case we might need them again in the future.

When he was writing this week's verse, Paul wanted readers to know that people are watching and making decisions about Jesus based on the attitudes and actions of His followers.

So we need to declutter. We need to toss the stuff that weighs us down and hurts our witness. But how? Thankfully, Paul told us how to do that, too: "We do this by keeping our eyes on Jesus, the champion who initiates and perfects our faith" (Hebrews 12:2).

That's it, isn't it? You and I can give our clutter and junk to Jesus, asking Him to help us focus our hearts and minds on the blessings we have through Him. We can be content and guilt-free, without worry or fear, knowing we are precious, cared for, and loved by Jesus, the One who makes our faith and hope-filled future possible. The One who enables us to live a clean life with a clear conscience. I'm ready to declutter! Are you?

Are you a spiritual hoarder? What clutter do you need to get rid of?

_____

_____

_____

_____

_____

Why do you think it's so hard to part with your particular brand of spiritual clutter?

_____

_____

_____

_____

_____

_____

People are making decisions about Jesus based on His followers' attitudes and actions. What do you want people to see in you?

_____

_____

_____

_____

_____

_____

Make a list of spiritual blessings like forgiveness, peace, strength, and hope. Say a prayer thanking God for making you His own and asking Him to help you declutter so you can focus on these blessings you have in Jesus.

_____

_____

_____

_____

_____

_____

_____

_____

_____

WHEN YOU'RE TIRED

Then Jesus said, "Come to me, all of you who are weary and carry heavy burdens, and I will give you rest."

MATTHEW 11:28

Are you tired? Weary from carrying your family's burdens? Exhausted by all that's going on in the world? Overworked? Drained? I often wonder if we accept being "tired" as just a part of our job description. We feel like we're not doing enough if we're not doing too much. Yet we feel guilty, too, because no matter how hard we try, we're still not getting everything done.

And that's the moment when Jesus holds out His hand and invites us to bring our burdens to Him, to give Him our worry, fear, and fatigue. He says, "Let Me take your confusion and chaos, and in its place I will give you My healing grace, perfect peace, and unfailing love. I took every part of your messed-up past to the cross. I died to save you and everyone who has ever lived from sin, death, and the evil enemy's power. So come to Me!"

There's something more. Jesus's invitation is not just about our past burdens; it is also a promise for today and tomorrow. In Matthew 11:29–30, He says, "Take my yoke upon you. Let me teach you, because I am humble and gentle at heart, and you will find rest for your souls. For my yoke is easy to bear, and the burden I give you is light."

It's a promise that offers us a better way to live, one that helps us know when to say no and when to turn off the news or take a break from social media. It's the promise that is able to give us strength, courage, hope, peace, and everything else we need to accomplish God's will. Because it reminds us that we are connected to Jesus, the One we can always trust to help us carry our burdens.

What does Jesus's invitation in today's Scripture mean to you?

_____

_____

_____

_____

_____

_____

Be honest: Are you trying to do too much, carrying burdens and concerns that you need to take to Jesus? If so, what are they?

_____

_____

_____

_____

_____

How can you set better boundaries and get the rest you need?

_____

_____

_____

_____

_____

_____

_____

Take some of the specific responses you wrote for the previous question and write a prayer asking God to help you know when to say no, when to ask for help, and when to simply take a break and rest.

_____

_____

_____

_____

_____

_____

_____

UNITED IN LOVE THROUGH CHRIST

For he himself is our peace, who has made the two groups one and has destroyed the barrier, the dividing wall of hostility.
EPHESIANS 2:14 (NIV)

In a time when we can identify everything about everyone through a DNA test, labeling based on identity seems more prevalent than ever. It often assumes that people of the same age, gender, race, religion, socioeconomic status, and/or education act, think, and believe as one.

But there are two truths from Scripture that completely contradict this divisive thinking. First, the Bible says that every person who ever lived is unique and wonderfully complex: "You made all the delicate, inner parts of my body and knit me together in my mother's womb. Thank you for making me so wonderfully complex" (Psalm 139:13–14). The marvelous truth is that you are God's one-of-a-kind creation. The only way we're all the same is that we are all human and all sinners. Every other label is unnecessary. You and every other person on earth is uniquely created with specific gifts and abilities to love God and glorify Him by loving and caring for all the other wonderfully unique people He created.

Second, Jesus died to destroy the barrier that labels and divides people: "Just as our bodies have many parts and each part has a special function, so it is with Christ's body. We are many parts of one body, and we all belong to each other" (Romans 12:4–5). Jesus repeatedly told His followers to love people in need, people who were different, people who didn't think like them. He even said, "I say, love your enemies! Pray for those who persecute you! In that way, you will be acting as true children of your Father in heaven" (Matthew 5:44–45).

May we cherish our unique individuality as we celebrate that we are united in love through Christ!

Have you ever been hurt because you were treated unfairly based on your external identity? Have you ever reacted to someone simply because of the label they wear?

_____

_____

_____

_____

How are you different from the people you know who live in your neighborhood or go to your church? How are you the same?

_____

_____

_____

_____

Make a list of ways you can use your unique gifts and abilities to love people who are different from you, remembering we are all "different" by His grace for His glory.

_____

_____

_____

_____

_____

_____

_____

Write a prayer asking God to help you see how wonderfully unique He made everyone around you. Ask Him to help you make a difference in your family and community by loving everyone like Jesus.

_____

_____

_____

_____

_____

_____

_____

WHEN FORGIVING IS HARD

*Make allowance for each other's faults, and forgive
anyone who offends you. Remember, the Lord forgave
you, so you must forgive others.*

COLOSSIANS 3:13

Who's the person you find it hardest to forgive? I know someone came to mind—someone always does.

I find it easy to forgive most of the time. When a person
with whom I have a solid relationship does or says something
thoughtless but then quickly apologizes, it's easy for me to let
it go and just move on. But when the painful consequences are
life-changing or the behavior is repeated again and again . . .
well, that's when forgiveness gets hard.

The thing is, God's Word to us about forgiveness doesn't
come with qualifiers. It doesn't say, "You must forgive others
unless they were being really mean," or "You must forgive
others unless it would be very difficult." In fact, Jesus said
more than once that the Father's forgiveness and ours go hand
in hand: "Forgive others, and you will be forgiven" (Luke 6:37).
Why? Why does God make forgiving others critically important in the life of His children?

Because He knows that bitterness and resentment in any
form make it almost impossible for us to love the way He
wants us to. On the other hand, when you and I forgive the
unthinkable, we show the world God's undeserved forgiveness

and love—and we open ourselves to His peace and freedom. Peace to let go of the past and freedom to heal.

When we refuse to forgive, on the other hand, we end up with the opposite of peace and freedom. In his book *Life Without Lack*, Dallas Willard writes, "The person who has the most power over your life is the person you have not forgiven." So this is the perfect time to surrender your struggle to forgive and give the power over your life to God, the One who gives you the freedom to live and love, forgiven and forgiving.

Who do you have a hard time forgiving? Acknowledge the pain you feel and admit your struggle.

_____

_____

_____

_____

_____

Why is forgiveness important to you? Why is it important that God forgives you, that other people forgive you, and that you can forgive them?

_____

_____

_____

_____

_____

Choose to forgive the person or people who hurt you. You can use the following if you need help:

Because I am completely loved, accepted, and forgiven by God in Christ Jesus, I have what I need to forgive you, _____, and I release you completely. I will no longer hold this against you. You are free. I am free.

_____

_____

_____

_____

_____

_____

_____

Talk to God about forgiveness—how it's hard sometimes, how you're thankful that He has forgiven you, and how you need His help to forgive those who have hurt you.

_____

_____

_____

_____

_____

_____

_____

WEEK 41

DRY BONES

The Lord took hold of me, and I was carried away by the Spirit of the Lord to a valley filled with bones.
EZEKIEL 37:1

Do you have hopes and dreams you've given up on and left for dead? Self-help books want us to believe that all we have to do is have a dream, set goals, and take steps to accomplish those goals, and ultimately we'll reach our objective. Simple, right? But sometimes progress feels impossible and our dreams seem lifeless.

That's why one of my favorite accounts in Scripture is the "valley of dry bones" in Ezekiel 37. In this passage, the "Spirit of the Lord" takes Ezekiel to a hillside overlooking a valley covered in scattered, dried-out old bones, and asks, "Son of man, can these bones become living people again?" I love Ezekiel's reply: "O Sovereign Lord, You alone know the answer to that" (Ezekiel 37:3). Essentially, he's saying, "I don't know. You alone hold the power over life and death, over creatures and creation, over hopes and dreams."

Then the Lord says, "Dry bones, listen to the word of the Lord! . . . I will put breath into you, and you will come to life. Then you will know that I am the Lord" (Ezekiel 37:4, 6). The Lord is able to breathe life into dry bones and dead dreams. He is able to heal and restore whatever He chooses for His glory.

So whatever your dreams are, surrender them to God. Trust His power to breathe life into whatever He chooses. Invite Him to work in and through you, use you for His glory, and give you His peace while you wait on His perfect timing.

What are some of the hopes and dreams you've given up and left in the metaphorical valley of dry bones?

_____

_____

_____

_____

_____

_____

_____

What does the conversation between the Lord and Ezekiel mean to you in light of your own abandoned hopes and dreams?

_____

_____

_____

_____

_____

_____

_____

In what way might God be breathing new life into you when it comes to your faith?

_____

_____

_____

_____

_____

_____

_____

Write down your hopes and dreams on the following lines and ask God to give you everything you need to pursue what He wants for you, even if it means waiting patiently while He works in your life.

_____

_____

_____

_____

_____

_____

_____

LIVE WITHOUT FEAR

*I know the Lord is always with me. I will not be
shaken, for he is right beside me.*
PSALM 16:8

How proficient are your fear-fighting skills? Personally, I
spent too many years working on my fear-feeling skills rather
than my fear-fighting skills. I believed if certain things happened, I wouldn't be equipped to handle them. So when I came
face-to-face with my greatest fears, it turned out . . . I was
right. I couldn't handle them.

But by His grace, God showed me I didn't have to "handle"
anything because He would help me. He assured me through
His Word and times of prayer that He would give me everything I needed to face each day.

He showed me verses like:

- **"God is our refuge and strength, always ready to
  help in times of trouble" (Psalm 46:1).**
- **"You will keep in perfect peace all who trust in you,
  all whose thoughts are fixed on you" (Isaiah 26:3).**
- **"My health may fail, and my spirit may grow weak,
  but God remains the strength of my heart; he is
  mine forever" (Psalm 73:26).**

What I learned about myself and fear was this: I believed I needed the strength to endure forever when the truth was I only needed to trust God to give me what I needed in the present moment. I learned the absolute truth of Jesus's words: "Seek the Kingdom of God above all else, and He will give you everything you need" (Luke 12:31). God showed me that when I need strength and courage or peace and patience, He will provide them!

And that made it possible for me to trust Him with my fears. God is faithful to keep His promises—always! And by His grace, you and I can say with confidence, "He is right beside me. I have everything I need to live without fear."

How often do you struggle with feelings of fear? How much does fear influence what you think, do, and say?

_____

_____

_____

_____

Write about a time when God helped you live through something that had previously frightened you.

_____

_____

_____

_____

_____

Take a moment to look up Romans 15:13, Psalm 23:4, Psalm 34:3–4, and Hebrews 13:8. Choose one or two you want to remember and write them here.

_____

_____

_____

_____

_____

_____

_____

What frightens you today? Write about it, and then talk with God about your struggle with fear and desire to trust Him to give you what you need, one moment at a time.

_____

_____

_____

_____

_____

_____

_____

_____

_____

GOD WILL USE YOUR STORY

Now all glory to God, who is able, through his mighty
power at work within us, to accomplish infinitely
more than we might ask or think.

EPHESIANS 3:20

I will always remember the day my friend looked at me and said, "Now you have a story. Your life looked too perfect before, but now . . ."

My "but now" story was an uncomfortable mess. I didn't really want to share it. I was a pastor's wife. I'd always been a firstborn people pleaser, a good girl. It's not that I felt prideful or "better than"—far from it. I was just very careful about the things I shared publicly. "But now," I no longer had a choice. This mess was out there for everyone to see, and my friend encouraged me to let God use it for His glory.

We live in a time when social media allows us to present whatever image we choose, and many of us stick to posting perfect family photos in far-off places. But what if we humbly talked about our lack of perfection and admitted our need for the power of God's transforming grace, mercy, and love? What if we confessed that He is still working on us rather than acting like we have our acts together?

Only you have your story, a story God can use to shine the light of His love. I've learned we don't have to share every gory detail. Remember Paul's "thorn in the flesh" (2 Corinthians 12:7)?

I think the Holy Spirit encouraged Paul to be less than specific about it in order to make it possible for you to see your "thorn" and for me to see mine.

So tell people how God has forgiven you, how He has seen you through a difficult time or is helping you find freedom from fear, anxiety, pride, impatience, anger, and so on. We all have struggles and imperfections. And by His grace, God is not only willing and able to help us and heal us; He is also willing and able to use our stories to accomplish more than we can imagine, all for His glory!

Write about a time when you were blessed by someone who shared their story of God's grace with you.

_____

_____

_____

_____

_____

What's your story of God's grace? What messy situation did He help you through?

_____

_____

_____

_____

_____

_____

How might you be able to glorify God and bless someone else by encouraging them with your story?

_____

_____

_____

_____

_____

_____

_____

Consider those you know who are going through a difficult struggle and write a prayer asking God to give you wisdom to share your story in ways that will bless them and give Him glory.

_____

_____

_____

_____

_____

_____

_____

TRULY HUMBLE AND HAPPY

The humble will see their God at work and be glad.
Let all who seek God's help be encouraged.

PSALM 69:32

One of Rev's favorite questions to ask a group study is: "Who do you think about more than anyone else?" Typically people say their kids, their spouse, or their boyfriend/girlfriend. He smiles, shakes his head, and says, "I don't think so. Unless you're unlike everyone else in the world, the person you think about most is . . . you!" (Picture the group sheepishly laughing and nodding.)

There's another thing that's true: The more we think about ourselves, the more miserable we are. I believe that's why the Bible makes a connection between humility and happiness. You see, the number one thing I've learned about humility is that truly humble people don't think they're humble! In fact, they don't think about themselves much at all. But they do have the following things in common1

1. **They focus their hearts and minds on the Lord (Isaiah 26:3).**

2. **They are overwhelmed by God's grace, mercy, and love (2 John 1:33**

3. They want to live out God's plans and purposes for them (Luke 10:274.

4. They are unique, content, and don't compare themselves with anyone else (Romans 3:235.

5. They do their best to love and serve others with kindness (Galatians 5:13).

One more thing: It's really hard to be truly humble. Our human nature wants us to focus on ourselves and compare ourselves with others. But the God we serve invites us to accept what we need from Him to be truly humble and happy.

And the good news is that if constantly thinking about ourselves makes us miserable, then living humbly and seeing God at work in us and through us has the power to make us happy.

Did you realize the true answer to Rev's favorite question before you read this devotion? Why do you think everyone tends to think about themselves the most?

_____

_____

_____

What part of being truly humble is hardest for you?

_____

_____

_____

_____

_____

Why do you think being truly humble has the power to make you happy?

_____

_____

_____

_____

_____

_____

If you're like me, your thoughts about yourself can be negative. Think about a specific area of your life where this is true for you and write a prayer asking God to help you focus on Him and others so you can experience the happiness found in humility.

_____

_____

_____

_____

_____

_____

_____

THE BLESSING OF ENCOURAGEMENT

May God, who gives this patience and encouragement,
help you live in complete harmony with each other,
as is fitting for followers of Christ Jesus.

ROMANS 15:5

I was hurrying through the store recently when I passed a younger woman going the opposite direction. Our eyes met, and we smiled. But then as she passed me, she said, "You are so pretty!" What?! I didn't feel pretty. I felt old, tired, and distracted. When I regained my composure, I turned and thanked her profusely. Her kind words blessed and encouraged me for days.

Did you know when you encourage someone, you're actually inspiring them with courage? The opposite is true as well: When you discourage someone, you're sucking the courage right out of them. No wonder it's hard to get out of bed when we feel discouraged!

But God's Word says that when you and I honestly take our feelings to Him, He will help us. David said it so well in Psalm 138: "As soon as I pray, you answer me; you encourage me by giving me strength" (Psalm 138:3).

And just like His love, God gives us more than enough encouragement to share with each other. I think that's the way it's supposed to work. Paul wrote that God gives His children the patience and encouragement they need to live in harmony with each other. He gives us what we need to live united in faith.

You and I can be each other's cheerleaders, like that young woman at the store was for me. We can inspire each other with a kind word, a helpful hand, or a listening ear. And one of the best things about God's encouragement plan is that the more we encourage others, the more we are encouraged ourselves. I want to be a courage inspirer. What about you?

Are you discouraged? What is discouraging you?

_____

_____

_____

_____

_____

Write about a time you were able to reach a goal because someone encouraged you.

_____

_____

_____

_____

_____

How might you use your God-given gifts and abilities to encourage someone who is discouraged?

_____

_____

_____

_____

_____

_____

_____

Make a list of people you want to encourage this week and start your encouragement of them by blessing them with prayer.

_____

_____

_____

_____

_____

_____

_____

_____

WALK-ON-WATER FAITH

*"Yes, come," Jesus said. So Peter went over the
side of the boat and walked on the water toward
Jesus. But when he saw the strong wind and
the waves, he was terrified and began to sink.
"Save me, Lord!" he shouted.*

MATTHEW 14:29–30

I can often be like Peter. One moment, I'm on a spiritual high,
completely focused on Jesus, jumping out of the boat with full
faith. The next, I'm distracted by choppy water splashing my
ankles, and before I know it, I'm sinking in fear.

The exchange between Jesus and Peter gives me hope
because it reminds me that although I may lose my focus
momentarily, Jesus is always there to help.

As Peter began to sink, he cried out, "Save me, Lord!"

What did Jesus do? He "immediately reached out and
grabbed Peter," saying, "You have so little faith" (Matthew 14:31).
I don't picture Jesus being stern or even disappointed in this
moment. I imagine Him with a twinkle in His eye, reaching out
with love and compassion.

I believe if the opportunity came again, Peter would jump
out of the boat in a holy heartbeat. He'd have courageous faith,
knowing Jesus was with him.

You and I can have walk-on-water faith, too—not because
we're strong and courageous on our own, but because Jesus

promised never to leave us or forsake us. He's always there to grab us when we cry out to Him for help.

Have you ever had a time when you felt so spiritually strong you felt like you had walk-on-water faith? Write about it.

_____

_____

_____

_____

_____

_____

What about a time when you were sinking with doubt? Did it help to know that Jesus was there to grab you when you cried out to Him for help?

_____

_____

_____

_____

_____

_____

_____

How do you normally picture Jesus saying, "You have so little faith"? Does it change your perception of the scene to picture Him being gentle and compassionate?

_____

_____

_____

_____

_____

_____

_____

Is life currently hard? Are you anxious about the future or sinking spiritually? Write a prayer asking Jesus for the walk-on-water faith you need to face each day with courage and strength.

_____

_____

_____

_____

_____

_____

_____

_____

GOD CALLS YOU "MINE"

Do not be afraid, for I have ransomed you.
I have called you by name; you are mine.
ISAIAH 43:1

When our oldest grandson was little and starting to assign names to the people in his life, he had his Momma, his Nana and Granddaddy, and his Gram and Grandpa. But whenever he got to his daddy, he simply called him "mine."

I don't think there is anything more personal or precious than being called someone's "mine." We all want that, don't we?

But relationships don't always go the way we want. Sometimes people betray, reject, or even leave us, and that piece of our heart defined by "mine" gets broken. I wonder, though, if maybe our imperfect relationships aren't supposed to be able to fill the "mine" piece of our heart. Maybe that piece is supposed to be filled by God Himself.

And Jesus made it possible: "The Son of Man came not to be served but to serve others and to give his life as a ransom for many" (Matthew 20:28). Jesus calls you "mine" as well. As Revelation 3:5 says, "I will never erase their names from the Book of Life, but I will announce before my Father and his angels that they are mine."

We can love and trust the One who is perfect and will always love us perfectly. The One who calls us "mine," no matter who we are, where we live, what we have, or what we've done. He told us to come to Him with humble thanks, praise, and trusting love (Matthew 11:28). He will fill our heart with perfect peace and lasting love because He will never fail or forsake us (Deuteronomy 31:8). And He will forever and always call us His very own.

Write Isaiah 43:1 here, replacing the word *you* with your name.

_____

_____

_____

_____

_____

_____

How does it make you feel to know that God calls you "mine" and has written your name in the Book of Life?

_____

_____

_____

_____

_____

_____

How can you make your relationships with people a reflection of your relationship with God, the One who calls you "mine"?

_____

_____

_____

_____

_____

_____

_____

What does it mean to you that Jesus will never leave you or forsake you? Tell Him about it in prayer.

_____

_____

_____

_____

_____

_____

_____

_____

HEALING YOUR BROKEN HEART

He heals the brokenhearted and bandages their
wounds. He counts the stars and calls them all by
name. How great is our Lord! His power is absolute!
His understanding is beyond comprehension.

PSALM 147:3–5

Someone broke a promise and cheated—again. Someone rejected your love and walked away. Someone you trusted betrayed you. And your heart is broken.

Having a broken heart means you're suffering from sorrow or grief so overwhelming it feels like you can't go on. If you've ever had a broken heart, you know the lingering pain feels like it will never go away.

But I want you to know it will. You will get through this. You have a promise from the Lord, the One who heals broken hearts. He created the stars and calls them by name. He created you and knows everything about you. And He understands what you're going through and promises to bring healing to your pain.

How do I know? Because He healed mine, and I'd love to tell you about the things God used to help me heal. He used quiet times of prayer to comfort me, heal my heart, and give me peace. He used His Word and His promises. Promises like

Philippians 4:13, Isaiah 41:10, Lamentations 3:22, and Psalm 55:22. He used the guidance of His Spirit to help me forgive the past and focus on the present. He used His all-sufficient grace to give me the strength to get out of bed and live each day.

He understands our pain because He experienced it. Jesus was betrayed, rejected, lied about, denied, and put to death. Nothing that happens to you or me in this broken world is beyond His care and understanding. So go to God with your past or present brokenhearted pain, and trust Him to heal your wounds and give you His all-sufficient grace, perfect peace, and lasting happiness.

What have you learned about yourself since having your heart broken?

_____

_____

_____

_____

How does it help you to know that Jesus experienced the pain of rejection and betrayal?

_____

_____

_____

_____

How might this experience help your faith grow?

_____

_____

_____

_____

_____

_____

_____

_____

Write a prayer thanking Jesus for being willing to experience the pain of betrayal and rejection. Ask God to heal your pain and give you hope for the future.

_____

_____

_____

_____

_____

_____

_____

_____

HIS PERFECT PEACE

"I am leaving you with a gift—peace of mind and heart. And the peace I give is a gift the world cannot give. So don't be troubled or afraid."

JOHN 14:27

If I asked you to rate your sense of peace on a scale of 1 to 10, with 1 being utter turmoil and 10 being perfect peace, what would you choose?

Years ago, I would have said I was about a 4—and that would have been on a good day. I wanted peace but typically felt it was just a few inches beyond my reach. My overscheduled planner, my family's needs, and my what-if worries made me wonder if I could ever truly experience the kind of peace the Bible said Jesus wanted me to have.

If peace of mind and heart was a gift from Jesus, why wasn't He giving it to me?

As I've talked to friends, I've realized I'm not the only one who struggles with this. I think I've figured out the problem. It's found in the words that follow Jesus's promise of peace in this week's Scripture: "The peace I give is a gift the world cannot give."

You and I can't try to do it all—make everyone happy, fix every problem, and plan for every potential predicament—and experience God's peace. It simply will not happen!

It's not about trying to solve the world's problems or even all our personal problems. It's about trusting God to guide us. It's inviting Him to help us do His will and love His people the way He wants us to. So let's take some time this week to surrender our schedules, families, and worries to Jesus, asking Him to replace our do-it-all inner turmoil with His perfect peace.

How would you describe perfect peace? Have you experienced moments of perfect peace?

_____

_____

_____

_____

_____

Make a list of your greatest areas of frustration right now—things you believe are up to you to do or fix, even if they might not be.

_____

_____

_____

_____

_____

_____

Are there things on your list that you could surrender?

_____

_____

_____

_____

_____

_____

_____

Write a prayer giving all your frustrations to Jesus and inviting Him to replace your anxiety with His peace.

_____

_____

_____

_____

_____

_____

_____

_____

HE HEARS YOUR CRIES

The Lord is righteous in everything he does; he is filled with kindness. The Lord is close to all who call on him, yes, to all who call on him in truth. He grants the desires of those who fear him; he hears their cries for help and rescues them.

PSALM 145:17–19

I'll never forget the birth of our firstborn. The last night I spent in the hospital, my nurse suggested that our sweet girl spend a few hours in the nursery so I could get some much-needed rest. But I couldn't relax. On a floor filled with moms and newborns, I could hear my daughter crying. And this momma's heart had to act. So I walked down the hall to the nursery, knocked on the door, and said, "I think I hear my baby crying." The nurse smiled and handed me my very unhappy, red-faced, teary-eyed little one. I will always remember watching her relax against my chest as she settled in next to my heart knowing she was loved and safe.

God hears your voice. It is not just another voice in the crowd to your Heavenly Father. Of all the voices in the world crying out to Him, He knows your name and hears your specific cries. Isaiah wrote down God's promise to the children of Israel: "Do not be afraid, for I have ransomed you. I have called you by name; you are mine" (Isaiah 43:1). I believe those words are true for each of God's children. He sent Jesus to pay the price necessary to deliver us from the consequences of our sins. That is the definition of love and kindness.

When you and I cry out to Him for forgiveness, peace, help, understanding, or anything else, the Lord hears us and comes to give us what we need. I couldn't leave my daughter to cry alone in the nursery. I love her too much not to want to soothe her and meet her needs. And I'm not even close to being a perfect parent—but God is! He is our perfect Heavenly Father, who will always and forever do what is best for His children when they cry out to Him.

Write about a time when God showed you that He is your loving Father who hears your cries and comes to comfort you.

_____

_____

_____

_____

_____

How does it make you feel to know that God hears your cries?

_____

_____

_____

_____

_____

How can this help you feel safe and secure as you think about any problems you might face in the future?

Write down whatever is weighing on your heart and mind right now. Then cry out to God and ask Him to help you trust Him to give you everything you need.

THE BLESSINGS OF GRATITUDE

Always be joyful. Never stop praying. Be thankful in all circumstances, for this is God's will for you who belong to Christ Jesus.
1 THESSALONIANS 5:16–18

Rev has a saying, one he started using during the 18 months he was sick with constrictive pericarditis: "If I wait until I feel good and life looks perfect to be thankful and happy, I may never be thankful and happy again."

I have to admit, I marveled at his attitude. His heart was being squeezed by a hard shell that was supposed to be his pericardial sac. His body retained extra liters of fluid that compressed his lungs and made it hard to breathe. But every day he got out of bed, thanked God for the day, and looked for reasons to be joyful.

I don't remember either of us being thankful for his illness, but I do remember being thankful for doctors, for friends who were praying, and for moments of fun that distracted us. And I think that's the point: We tried to keep our gaze fixed on the positive.

It's easy to become so focused on a problem that we lose our joy and gratitude. But when we pray about a problem and entrust it to God, we can focus on what He is doing both in us and in those around us. Every single day, no matter how difficult our circumstances, "[we] know that God causes everything to work together for the good of those who love God" (Romans 8:28). And His goodness invites the following response from us: "Everything comes from him and exists by his power and is intended for his glory. All glory to him forever! Amen" (Romans 11:36).

Whatever your struggle, give it to God in prayer and trust Him to reveal reasons to be joyful and grateful.

When is it hardest for you to live out God's will of prayer, joy, and gratitude?

_____

_____

_____

_____

_____

Has God ever helped you be joyful and thankful even though you were going through something difficult and painful?

_____

_____

_____

_____

_____

_____

What does it mean to you that God is at work in and around you for your good and His glory?

_____

_____

_____

_____

_____

_____

_____

Write a list of your current struggles; then write the name of Jesus over the top. Finally, below or next to your list, write a prayer asking Him to help you trust Him and live with gratitude and joy.

_____

_____

_____

_____

_____

_____

_____

_____

MY LIFE VERSE

*My health may fail, and my spirit may
grow weak, but God remains the strength
of my heart; he is mine forever.*

PSALM 73:26

I was grieving. My heart was broken, and my spirit was weak.
I desperately needed God to be my strength. Then I read
Psalm 73:25: "Whom have I in heaven but you? I desire you
more than anything on earth." I cried out in prayer through
tears, "God, I need You! More than anything else in the world!"

The next verse reads, "My health may fail, and my spirit
may grow weak, but God remains the strength of my heart; He
is mine forever." As I read it, I felt the Lord saying, "I love you.
However weak you are in body or spirit, I will give you the
strength you need."

And I received the promise. I believed God cared about me
right where I was at that moment, crushed and fragile. I felt
His love, and for the first time, I knew I could truly trust Him
with every part of my life no matter what I was going through.
I gave Him my failures and brokenness, my good-girl pride,
and my fear and anxiety. In return, He gave me forgiveness,
peace, strength, and so much more.

That's why I claim Psalm 73:26 as my "life verse." It has
become my constant reminder that no matter what's going on

in my life, my loving Heavenly Father will give me what I need to help me handle it.

You can depend on His promises, too. I encourage you to claim your own life verse and memorize it. Ask Jesus to be the Lord of your life and surrender everything to Him. You can trust Him to give you whatever you need because He loves you. He will be the strength of your heart. He wants to be yours forever.

In what ways are you feeling physically or emotionally weak?

_____

_____

_____

_____

_____

What does it mean to you that God is "yours forever"? How has God shown up for you when you needed Him most?

_____

_____

_____

_____

_____

_____

_____

Write your life verse here. If you don't have one, consider Psalm 73:26. Or research Scripture by topic to find a verse that makes you heart feel protected and try it out.

_____

_____

_____

_____

_____

_____

_____

Tell God about your desire to surrender every part of your life to Him, inviting Him to strengthen you and give you the peace only He can offer.

_____

_____

_____

_____

_____

_____

_____

_____

REFERENCES

Elliot, Elisabeth. *Passion and Purity: Learning to Bring Your Love Life Under Christ's Control*. Grand Rapids, MI: Baker Publishing Group, 2002.

Willard, Dallas. *Life Without Lack: Living in the Fullness of Psalm 23*. Nashville, TN: Thomas Nelson, 2018.

ACKNOWLEDGMENTS

Every book project requires a team to take it from conception to completion, and I am so thankful for the wonderful people who helped make this project a beautiful reality.

Thank you to everyone who prayed for and encouraged me throughout this process. I have felt your love, and God used you to lift my spirits and brighten my days.

I am so very thankful for all my blogger friends who inspire me and give me so much joy. Thank you for being the best cheerleaders and prayer partners a girl can have. I love you all.

Blessings and big hugs to my launch team and those of you who have helped me spread the word about this devotional journal. Thank you for posting, pinning, sharing, and announcing this book so enthusiastically.

Thank you to the wonderful team at Rockridge Press. And special thanks to Lauren O'Neal for her helpful suggestions and kind encouragement. You are truly a blessing.

A huge hug and thank-you to my husband, "Rev." You have always believed in me, even when I have doubted myself. Thank you for your constant support, ideas, and wise advice. I thank the Lord for you.

And finally, thanks and praise to my Lord and Savior, Jesus, for helping me know the truth that when I seek Him first, He really will give me everything I need.

ABOUT THE AUTHOR

 **DEB WOLF** is a speaker, writer, and teacher with a degree in education. A blogger for more than 12 years, she's currently writing at CountingMyBlessings.com, where she encourages her readers to focus on what God is doing at the intersection of faith and life. She loves telling people how God is patiently and persistently taking her from the fearful "good little church girl" she used to be and helping her trust His promises and experience a life inspired by His strength, courage, peace, and joy. Deb is a blessed wife, mom, gram, daughter, sister, and friend who loves babies, puppies, chocolate, coffee, laughter, and telling everyone she meets about the blessings of grace, mercy, and love she has found in Jesus.

CPSIA information can be obtained
at www.ICGtesting.com
Printed in the USA
JSHW031502130122
21972JS00007B/228